To Nesta, my best little buddy,
who has taught me to love picture books.
                    —JLP   To my daughter, Maria Mendoza.
                                              —GM

Colors of the Wind
The Story of Blind Artist and Champion Runner
George Mendoza

by J.L. Powers

paintings by George Mendoza

drawings by Hayley Morgan-Sanders

Purple House Press   Kentucky

George *never* stayed still.
When I grow up, he thought,
I will be a basketball player.

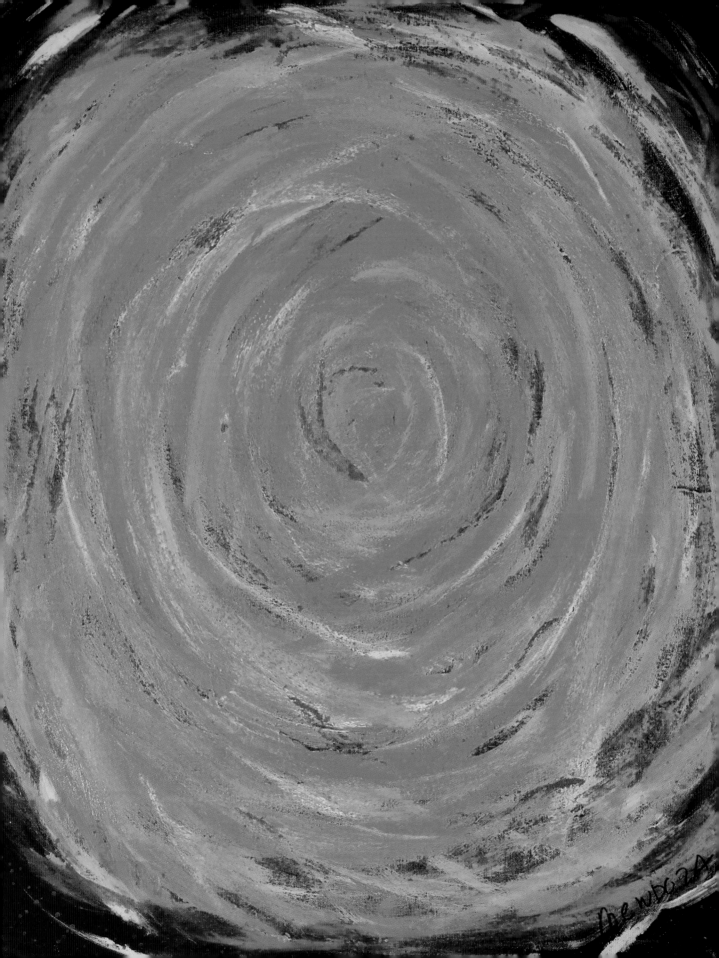

George *never* got sick.
But one day, he looked out the window
and saw the whole world painted red.
He thought, *That's funny.*

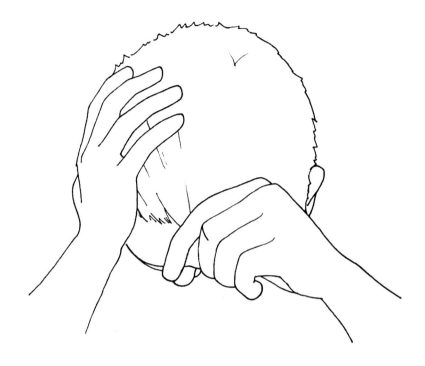

George *never* fumbled the basketball.
But then he started to see
blue and orange and yellow squiggles
floating in the air
instead of the basket
whenever he tried to make a shot.
His head hurt. All the time.
Sometimes, it hurt so bad, he had to stay in bed all day
and he couldn't play basketball.
He thought, *That isn't so funny.*

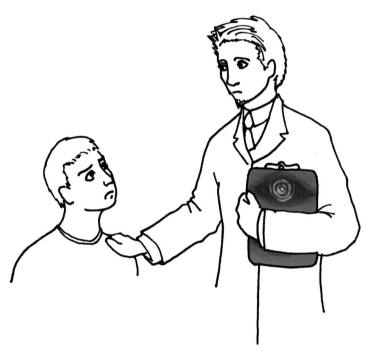

The doctor said,
"George, you're going blind."
George didn't lose all his sight, though.
Instead, he started seeing flashing lights and brilliant colors
even at night when he dreamed.
He tried shooting baskets, but he kept missing.
Instead of a basket, he saw an enormous eye
floating in the air.

George and his mother moved to New Mexico
where the sun always shines.
The sun helped George's headaches
but he was still clumsy.
Whenever he tripped over something
that everybody else could see,
he yelled at himself.

At a camp for the blind,
George and Debbie went for a walk.
Debbie had been blind from birth.
She had never seen the mountains
or a Ferris Wheel.
When the wind ruffled her hair,
she asked, "What color is the wind?"
George looked around at what he saw
and answered, "The wind is like a rainbow.
It has every color in the world."

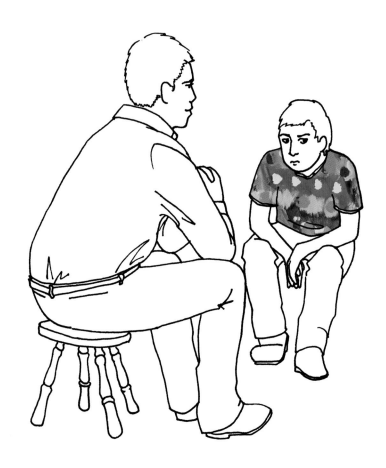

George soon forgot Debbie's question.
"Nobody else sees the way you do," a priest told him.
"You should paint what you see."
George didn't listen.
He thought, *I'll never be able to do*
what everybody else can do.

That was when George started to run.
Running made him so tired,
he forgot about being blind.
That was one of the reasons he liked to run.

George discovered he could run very fast.
He could run a mile faster than any other blind person.
In fact, he ran so fast,
he went to the Olympics. Twice.

But no matter how far or how fast he ran,
George always saw things
that nobody else could see.
When he looked at the world,
it was like looking into a kaleidoscope.

El Santuario de Chimayó chapel

George's best friend died in a motorcycle accident.
The thought that he might die scared George.
He started to wonder, *Why am I even here?*
What's my purpose in life?

Sitting in a chapel one day, he saw something different
than the usual squiggles or brilliant colors floating in the air.
He saw himself, bathed in light, running.
He was running into the light.

George never forgot that vision.
Now he had something to say to people
when they asked him what it was like to be blind.
He kept running but started talking, too.
Sometimes he talked to crowds of people.
He told them that everybody was good at *something*.

One day, a flyer arrived in the mail,
advertising a contest for blind artists.
George remembered the priest, who told him,
"You should paint what you see."
He remembered Debbie's question from so many years ago.
He asked himself, "What color *is* the wind?"
George started to paint,
just like the priest told him to do.

George had recently hiked through a swarm of butterflies.
He painted what he saw and named it *Butterfly Eyes.*
It was his first painting.
He won the contest.
After that, he started painting every day.

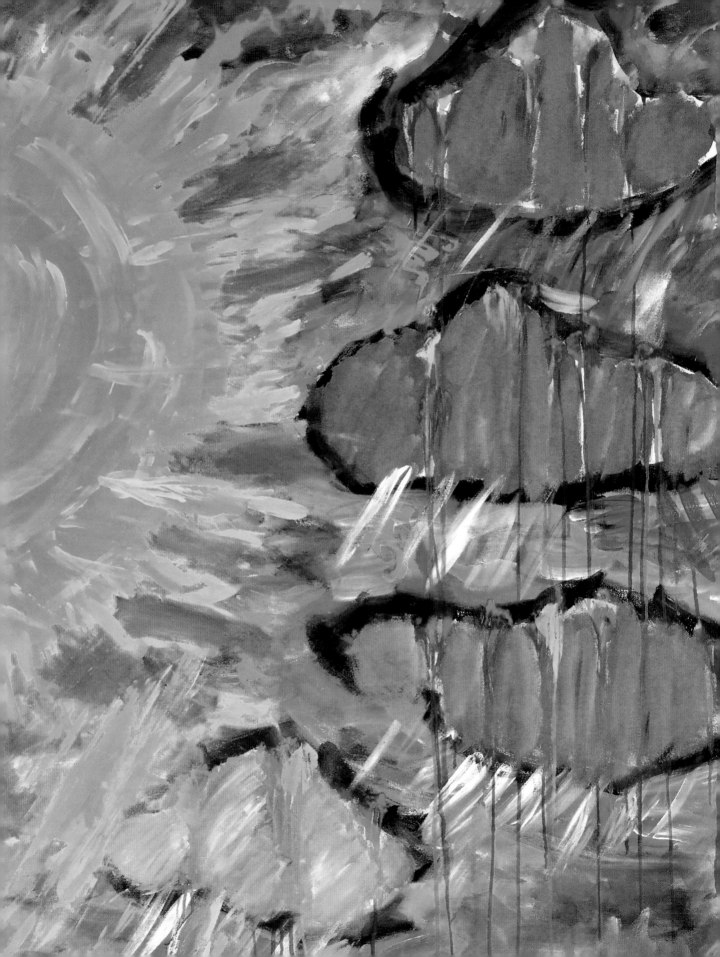

Sometimes, George experiments.
He might place a candle out in the wind or rain,
so he can see it flicker
when the wind blows or raindrops fall.
Then he paints all the eerie colors and strange things
he sees in the flames.

Sometimes, George uses paintbrushes.
But most days, he fingerpaints,
using heavy work gloves
with gobs and gobs of paint.

Sometimes, George visits schools to talk with students.
He asks them the same question every time.
He asks, "What color is the wind?"
Then he lets them paint.
Their paintings always surprise him.

Sometimes, George still runs.
But when he looks at all the paintings
stacked in his studio,
hung on the walls of his house
or, even better, inside a museum,
he smiles.
He never thought he would be an artist
when he grew up.

George Mendoza, Athlete and Artist

George Mendoza, who has been legally blind since the age of 15, paints what he sees. This is possible only because he has a very rare form of blindness, called fundus flavimaculatus, which destroyed his central vision but left him with limited peripheral vision. He now has a condition that he refers to as "kaleidoscope eyes" because of the way objects are reflected back and multiplied in his vision.

"I lost 90% of my eyesight in a period from two days to six months," he says. "About six years later, I started seeing explosive colors, designs, and eyes looking at me. My brain is trying to tell my eyes what to see, but it can't, so it reports back these weird distortions. That's what I paint."

Because George never sees the same thing two days in a row, he says that affects his paintings as well. "If I get close to the canvas, I can still see what I did the day before," he says. "So I can paint from the memory of what I saw that inspired the painting, but each painting is an evolution. It builds upon the original vision but includes what I'm currently seeing."

If he gets involved enough in painting, he says, he's able to ignore the crazy things he's seeing. "They're there but I can focus and ignore them."

When he first started going blind and experiencing the constant visions, a priest in New Mexico suggested that George paint what he saw. At the time, however, he was obsessed with running, so he didn't pay much attention. "I never jumped on his advice because I was too busy with the Olympics. I was running 100 miles a week, so I was physically tired."

In March, 1980, George Mendoza set the world record for the mile by a blind runner, with a time of 4:28 and the national record for the half-mile with a time of 2:10. In June, 1980, he participated in the Olympics for the Disabled in Holland and placed fourth in the 1500-meter race. George returned to the Olympics in New York in 1984 and placed fourth in the 1500-meter race. To train, George ran cross-country in fields near where he lived.

It wasn't until his late thirties that George recalled the words of the priest. At the same time, a memory from his first years of blindness stoked his creativity. He had been at a summer camp for the blind and had gone for a walk with a little girl named Debbie, who had been blind since birth. When the breeze ruffled her

Training for the 1980 Olympics. George maintained his position by focusing on the white line at the outer edge of the track.

hair, lifting it from her forehead, she suddenly asked, "What color is the wind?" The memory of that little girl's question gave George the freedom to explore his blindness through the visual medium of painting.

"[Blind people] have a different imagination," George says. "I remember I met this one blind singer...His song described a tree in his backyard and he said it was 35 miles tall. I was just facing blindness, a 15-year-old kid, totally out of hope, and I run into Ken Medema who's telling me this tree is 35 miles tall. If you've never been able to see the wind or the shape of a tree, you're going to think the tree is that tall or the wind is full of colors. When I was at the New Mexico School for the Blind and Visually Impaired, this little boy had a Braille map of the world. He thought he could [walk] from New Mexico to New York in two hours. I've joined that world, whether I wanted to or not."

Photo by William Faulkner

George Mendoza's biography, *Running Toward the Light: The George Mendoza Story,* written by William J. Buchanan, was reissued by the University of New Mexico Press in 2006. *Vision of the Soul: The George Mendoza Story,* narrated by actor Robert Duvall, aired on PBS stations around the country in the summer of 2006. He has had art shows at museums in Texas, Colorado, New York, California and New Mexico. His exhibition *Colors of the Wind* is a National Smithsonian Affiliates traveling art exhibit. It has shown at the Irving Arts Center in Dallas and the Ellen Noël Art Museum in Odessa, Texas.

These days, George spends most of his days painting. Recently, some of his paintings have been used to create unusual designs on fabrics. He is now a very popular artist among quilters. In 2009, Westminster Fabrics of Charlotte, North Carolina licensed Mendoza's art to create a cotton fabric collection. The collection made its debut at the International Quilt Market. Mendoza's art has been distributed worldwide ever since.

George lives in Las Cruces, New Mexico. He is founder and president of the Wise Tree Foundation, Inc., a non-profit corporation for the promotion of the arts.

Titles of the paintings presented in this book.

1. Roadrunner Dreams
2. Blind Man Touching the Sun
3. Flaming Rose
4. Last Rays of the Sun
5. Visionary Eye
6. Land of Enchantment
7. Colors of the Wind
8. Black Magic Eye
9. Blazing Tree
10. Kaleidoscope Eyes
11. Here Comes the Sun
12. God's Heart
13. Butterfly Eyes
14. Bleeding Clouds
15. Purple Moon
16. Wise Tree
17. Red Mesa
Front cover: In Memory
    of Ray Charles
Back cover: Wise Tree

A tribute to paintings we love, but had no space to include.

Published by Purple House Press
an imprint of Purple House, Inc.
PO Box 787, Cynthiana, KY 41031
www.purplehousepress.com

Text copyright © 2014 by J.L. Powers
Paintings copyright © 2014 by George Mendoza
Drawings copyright © 2014 by Hayley Morgan-Sanders
The publisher thanks Tokind for photographing George Mendoza's work.

Library of Congress Cataloging-in-Publication Data

Powers, J.L. (Jessica Lynn), 1974– author.
    Colors of the wind : the story of blind artist and champion runner George Mendoza / by J.L. Powers; paintings by George Mendoza; drawings by Hayley Morgan-Sanders. — First Edition
        pages cm
        ISBN 978-1-930900-73-8 (hardcover : alk. paper)
1. Mendoza, George, 1955—Juvenile literature. 2. Blind artists—United States—Biography—Juvenile literature. 3. Blind athletes—United States—Biography—Juvenile literature. I. Mendoza, George, 1955– illustrator. II. Morgan-Sanders, Hayley, illustrator. III. Mendoza, George, 1955– Paintings. Selections. IV. Title.
        ND237.M4235P69 2014
        759.13—dc23
        2014001565

Printed in South Korea by PACOM
1 2 3 4 5 6 7 8 9 10
First Edition